BUILD YOUR SUCCESS STORY

Aadya L

BlueRose ONE.com DIY
Stories Matter
NewDelhi • London

BLUEROSE PUBLISHERS
India | U.K.

BlueRose ONE.com
Stories Matter
NewDelhi • London

For permissions requests or inquiries regarding this publication,
please contact:

BLUEROSE PUBLISHERS
www.BlueRoseONE.com
info@bluerosepublishers.com
+91 8882 898 898
+4407342408967

ISBN: 978-93-6261-455-1

First Edition: April 2024

Aadya Dr@ Pharm-D

Writer's introduction

Greetings,

My name is Aadya L, and I am a diligent pharmacy student who has undertaken the esteemed Doctor of Pharmacy program at Visveswarapura Institute of Pharmaceutical Sciences,KIMS affiliated with Rajive Gandhi University Of Health Science, Bangalore. With a passion for advancing healthcare and a commitment to academic excellence, I have dedicated myself to mastering the intricacies of pharmaceutical sciences and clinical practice.
Throughout my academic journey, I have immersed myself in a rigorous curriculum designed to cultivate a comprehensive understanding of pharmacology, therapeutics, and patient care.
My coursework has equipped me with the knowledge and skills necessary to navigate the complexities of modern healthcare delivery while emphasizing the importance of ethical conduct and patient-centered care.
In addition to my academic pursuits, I have actively engaged in extracurricular activities and volunteer initiatives aimed at enhancing my professional development and contributing the betterment of the community. These experiences have reinforced my dedication to serving others and have instilled in me a profound sense of responsibility as a future healthcare practitioner. As I continue my journey in pharmacy, I am eager to leverage my education, skills, and experiences to make meaningful contributions to the field of pharmacy and to positively impact the lives of those in need. I am committed to lifelong learning and growth, and I am enthusiastic about the opportunities that lie ahead in my career.

Thank you for considering my candidacy, and I look forward to the possibility of contributing to your esteemed organization.

Warm regards,

Acknowledgement

I would like to acknowledge the extraordinary depth...
I owe to the teachers who have guided me in the completion of this book.
I would not be able to get my work done without the continual support of my

FATHER: LAKSHMIKANTHA. R

and

MOTHER: KALAVATHI. K

PREFACE

In the narrative of my forthcoming book, I delve into the intricacies of my personal journey, highlighting not only the heights of success but also the depths of failure that have shaped my path. Through candid reflection and introspection, I offer invaluable insights and strategies gleaned from navigating both triumphs and setbacks. These experiences serve not only as a testament to my own growth but also as invaluable lessons for aspiring individuals on their quest for success. By embracing the wisdom born from both victory and defeat, I aim to empower and inspire the next generation of achievers to navigate life's challenges with resilience, determination, and unwavering resolve.

CONTENTS

1. Goal Setting

2. Time Management

3. Motivation and Mindset

4. Study Techniques

5. Note-taking Skills

6. Memory Improvement

7. Critical thinking and problem -solving

"THE ONLY WAY TO DO GREAT WORK IS TO LOVE WHAT YOU DO."

STEVE JOBS

TOPIC 1: GOAL SETTING

Discuss the importance of setting specific, measurable, achievable, relevant, and time-bound (SMART) goals for both short-term and long-term success.

some important tips for short term goals:

- Set specific, achievable objectives for the next few weeks or months.
- Break down larger tasks into smaller, manageable steps.
- Prioritize tasks based on urgency and importance.
- Set deadlines for each short-term goal to create a sense of urgency.
- Focus on actions that can be completed within a relatively short time frame.
- Review and reassess short-term goals regularly to ensure alignment with long-term objectives.
- Keep short-term goals realistic and manageable to maintain momentum.
- Use tools such as to-do lists, calendars, or task management apps to stay organized.
- Stay disciplined and focused on completing short-term tasks to move closer to your long-term goals.

some important tips for long term goals:

- Establish broader, more ambitious targets for the next several months or years.
- Outline a clear timeline or roadmap for achieving your long-term goals.
- Identify potential obstacles and develop strategies to overcome them.
- Monitor progress regularly and adjust goals as needed.
- Celebrate milestones and achievements along the way to maintain motivation.
- Stay flexible and open to adapting your plans based on changing circumstances.
- Stay committed to your long-term vision and remain persistent in pursuing it.
- Seek feedback and support from mentors, peers, or professionals to help you stay on track.
- Continuously invest in your personal and professional development to enhance your chances of long-term success.

By following these smart tips for goal setting, you can effectively plan and achieve both short-term and long-term success in your personal and professional endeavors.

"SUCCESS IS NOT FINAL, FAILURE IS NOT FATAL: IT IS THE COURAGE TO CONTINUE THAT COUNTS."

WINSTON CHURCHILL

TOPIC 2:

TIME MANAGEMENT

Offer strategies for effectively managing time, including prioritization, creating schedules, and minimizing distractions.

Time management is crucial for students to balance their academic responsibilities, extracurricular activities, and personal life effectively. Here are some rules and tips regarding time management for every student:

1. Set Priorities: Identify your most important tasks and prioritize them based on deadlines and importance.
2. Use a Planner or Calendar: Keep track of assignments, exams, and other commitments using a planner or digital calendar to stay organized.
3. Break Tasks into Smaller Steps: Break down larger tasks into smaller, manageable steps to avoid feeling overwhelmed and make progress more manageable.

4. Set Realistic Goals: Set achievable goals for each study session or day to stay motivated and maintain momentum.
5. Create a Schedule: Allocate specific blocks of time for studying, attending classes, and participating in extracurricular activities to create a balanced schedule.
6. Limit Distractions: Minimize distractions such as social media, phone calls, or television while studying to maintain focus and productivity.
7. Use Time Blocks: Use the Pomodoro Technique or other time-blocking methods to work in focused intervals with short breaks in between.
8. Avoid Procrastination: Start tasks as soon as possible rather than waiting until the last minute to avoid unnecessary stress and rush.
9. Learn to Say No: Learn to say no to activities or commitments that don't align with your priorities or goals to avoid overcommitting yourself.
10. Take Breaks: Schedule regular breaks during study sessions to recharge and prevent burnout.
11. Stay Flexible: Be flexible and willing to adjust your schedule as needed to accommodate unexpected events or changes.
12. Practice Self-Care: Take care of your physical and mental health by getting enough sleep, eating well, exercising regularly, and managing stress effectively.

13. Review and Reflect: Reflect on how you're spending your time and adjust your schedule or habits accordingly to improve efficiency and effectiveness.
14. Seek Support: Don't hesitate to seek help from teachers, tutors, or classmates if you're struggling with time management or academic challenges.
15. Celebrate Progress: Celebrate your achievements and progress, no matter how small, to stay motivated and positive.

By implementing these rules and tips, students can better manage their time, reduce stress, and achieve greater success in their academic and personal lives.

"THE FUTURE BELONGS TO THOSE WHO BELIEVE IN THE BEAUTY OF THEIR DREAMS."

ELEANOR ROOSEVELT

TOPIC 3:

MOTIVATION AND MINDSET

Explore ways to cultivate a positive mindset, stay motivated, overcome procrastination, and maintain resilience in the face of challenges.

1. Find Your Why: Identify your reasons for pursuing your goals and remind yourself of them regularly to stay motivated.
2. Break Tasks into Manageable Steps: Break down larger tasks into smaller, more manageable steps to avoid feeling overwhelmed.
3. Create a Reward System: Reward yourself for completing tasks or reaching milestones to reinforce positive behavior.
4. Surround Yourself with Positive Influences: Surround yourself with supportive friends, family, and mentors who encourage and motivate you.
5. Visualize Success: Visualize yourself achieving your goals and imagine how it will feel, which can help boost motivation.

6. Stay Curious and Interested: Maintain a curiosity and interest in your studies by exploring topics that intrigue you and seeking out new challenges.
7. Seek Inspiration: Find inspiration from successful individuals, motivational quotes, or stories of perseverance to keep you inspired during challenging times.
8. Stay Positive: Focus on the positive aspects of your progress and experiences, and practice gratitude for what you've accomplished so far.
9. Learn from Setbacks: View setbacks and failures as opportunities for growth and learning rather than reasons to give up.
10. Stay Focused on the Present: Concentrate on what you can control and take action in the present moment rather than dwelling on past mistakes or worrying about the future.
11. Stay Flexible: Be adaptable and willing to adjust your plans or goals as needed based on changing circumstances or feedback.
12. Celebrate Progress: Celebrate your achievements and progress, no matter how small, to maintain motivation and momentum toward your goals.

"SUCCESS IS NOT THE KEY TO HAPPINESS. HAPPINESS IS THE KEY TO SUCCESS. IF YOU LOVE WHAT YOU ARE DOING, YOU WILL BE SUCCESSFUL."

ALBERT SCHWEITZER

TOPIC 4:

STUDY TECHNIQUES

Providing tips for effective studying, such as active learning methods, spaced repetition, and retrieval practice.

1. Active Reading: Engage with the material actively while reading by highlighting key points, taking notes, and asking questions to enhance understanding and retention.
2. Spaced Repetition: Review material at spaced intervals over time to reinforce learning and improve long-term retention.
3. Flashcards: Create flashcards to test yourself on key concepts, terms, and definitions, facilitating active recall and memory consolidation.
4. Practice Problems: Solve practice problems or questions related to the topic to apply theoretical knowledge and improve problem-solving skills.
5. Teach Others: Explain concepts to friends, family members, or classmates to reinforce understanding and identify areas of weakness.

6. Mind Mapping: Create visual representations of ideas, concepts, and relationships using mind maps to organize information and enhance comprehension.
7. Group Study: Collaborate with classmates to discuss and review material, share perspectives, and clarify doubts, promoting active learning and social interaction.
8. Summarization: Summarize complex information in your own words to condense and simplify the material, aiding comprehension and retention.
9. Chunking: Break down large amounts of information into smaller, more manageable chunks to facilitate learning and reduce cognitive overload.
10. Utilize Resources: Make use of textbooks, online resources, lecture notes, and supplementary materials to gain multiple perspectives and deepen understanding.
11. Stay Organized: Keep study materials, notes, and resources organized and easily accessible to minimize distractions and maximize productivity.
12. Set Specific Goals: Set clear, achievable study goals for each session to maintain focus and motivation.
13. Take Regular Breaks: Schedule short breaks during study sessions to rest and recharge, preventing burnout and maintaining concentration.

14. Use Mnemonics: Create mnemonic devices, acronyms, or rhymes to aid memorization and recall of complex information.
15. Review and Self-Assessment: Regularly review and test yourself on the material to identify areas of weakness and track progress over time.

By incorporating these effective study techniques into their routines, students can optimize their learning, improve retention, and achieve academic success.

"SUCCESS USUALLY COMES TO THOSE WHO ARE TOO BUSY TO BE LOOKING FOR IT."

HENRY DAVID THOREAU

TOPIC 5:

NOTE-TAKING SKILLS

Share techniques for taking concise, organized, and meaningful notes during lectures, readings, and study sessions.

1. Cornell Method: Divide your paper into three sections: a narrow column on the left for cues or questions, a wider column on the right for notes, and a bottom section for summarizing key points. Write main ideas and keywords in the right column, then add cues or questions in the left column and summarize the main points in the bottom section after the lecture or reading.
2. Outline Method: Organize notes in a hierarchical structure using bullet points or numbers to denote main ideas, subtopics, and supporting details. This method is especially useful for organizing complex information and understanding relationships between different concepts.
3. Mind Mapping: Create visual diagrams that depict relationships between ideas, concepts, and keywords using branches and nodes. Start with a central idea or topic and branch out to subtopics and related information, using colors, symbols, and images to enhance understanding and retention.

4. Charting Method: Use tables, grids, or charts to organize information into categories, comparisons, or timelines. This method is particularly effective for summarizing data, comparing different perspectives, or illustrating chronological sequences.

5. Sentence Method: Write notes in complete sentences, focusing on capturing key ideas, explanations, and examples. This method is beneficial for students who prefer writing in full sentences and paragraphs rather than using bullet points or abbreviations.

6. Mapping Method: Draw spatial representations of concepts, processes, or relationships using diagrams, flowcharts, or concept maps. This method helps visualize complex information and understand connections between different elements.

7. Abbreviations and Symbols: Develop a system of abbreviations, symbols, and shorthand to speed up note-taking and capture information efficiently. Use symbols for common words or phrases and abbreviate long words or phrases to save time.

8. Highlighting and Color Coding: Use highlighters, markers, or colored pens to emphasize important points, key terms, or headings. Color coding information helps organize notes visually and draws attention to essential concepts.

9. Annotating and Summarizing: Write annotations or summaries in the margins of your notes to provide context, explanations, or personal insights. Summarize key points at the end of each section or page to reinforce understanding and retention.

10. Digital Note-Taking Tools: Utilize digital note-taking apps or software such as Microsoft OneNote, Evernote, or Notion to organize, search, and annotate notes electronically. Digital tools offer flexibility, accessibility, and the ability to incorporate multimedia elements such as images, audio, and video.

Experiment with different note-taking methods to find the ones that work best for your learning style and preferences. Remember to review and revise your notes regularly to reinforce learning and prepare for exams or assignments.

"SUCCESS IS WALKING FROM FAILURE TO FAILURE WITH NO LOSS OF ENTHUSIASM."

WINSTON CHURCHILL

TOPIC 6: MEMORY IMPROVEMENT

Offer strategies for enhancing memory retention and recall, including mnemonic devices, visualization techniques, and memory palace methods.

1. Establish a Routine: Establish a consistent study routine and schedule regular study sessions to reinforce learning and develop a sense of familiarity with the material.
2. Use Mnemonics: Create mnemonic devices, acronyms, or rhymes to help remember complex information or sequences. Mnemonics leverage existing memory associations to aid recall.
3. Visualize Information: Visualize concepts, processes, or information in your mind's eye to create vivid mental images that can be easier to recall later. Associating information with visual imagery enhances memory retention.
4. Practice Retrieval: Actively retrieve information from memory by self-testing or quizzing yourself on key concepts. Testing your recall strengthens memory retrieval pathways and enhances retention.

5. Engage Multiple Senses: Engage multiple senses while studying by incorporating auditory, visual, and kinesthetic elements. Experiment with different study modalities such as reading, writing, listening, and hands-on activities to enhance memory encoding.
6. Get Enough Sleep: Prioritize sleep and aim for at least 7-8 hours of quality sleep per night. Sleep plays a crucial role in memory consolidation and cognitive function, so adequate rest is essential for optimal learning and memory.
7. Stay Active: Regular physical activity improves blood flow to the brain and enhances cognitive function, including memory. Incorporate regular exercise into your routine to support overall brain health and memory performance.
8. Manage Stress: Practice stress management techniques such as deep breathing, meditation, or mindfulness to reduce stress and anxiety, which can impair memory function. High levels of stress interfere with memory encoding and retrieval processes.
9. Stay Hydrated and Eat Well: Maintain a balanced diet and stay hydrated to support brain health and cognitive function. Certain nutrients, such as omega-3 fatty acids and antioxidants, are particularly beneficial for memory and brain health.

10. Stay Curious and Interested: Cultivate a genuine interest in the material you're studying to enhance motivation and engagement. Curiosity stimulates learning and memory processes, making information easier to retain.

11. Review and Reflect: Regularly review and reflect on the material you've learned to reinforce memory consolidation and identify areas for further review or clarification.

Incorporate these memory improvement tips into your study routine to enhance learning, retention, and academic performance. Experiment with different techniques to find the ones that work best for you.

TOPIC-7:

CRITICAL THINKING AND PROBLEM-SOLVING

Explore ways to develop critical thinking skills, analyze information critically, and solve problems effectively.

Critical thinking is the ability to analyze, evaluate, and synthesize information objectively and logically to form reasoned judgments and make informed decisions.

1. Importance in Competitive Exams: Critical thinking is a vital skill in competitive exams as it enables students to understand and interpret complex questions, identify relevant information, and apply effective problem-solving strategies to arrive at accurate solutions.
2. Analytical Skills: Competitive exams often require students to analyze data, passages, or scenarios to extract key information and draw logical conclusions. Developing strong analytical skills through practice and exposure to diverse problem-solving scenarios is essential.

3. Evaluation of Arguments: Students need to evaluate the validity and credibility of arguments, claims, or hypotheses presented in exam questions. They must identify logical fallacies, inconsistencies, or biases and assess the strength of evidence supporting various viewpoints.
4. Problem-Solving Strategies: Effective problem-solving involves breaking down complex problems into smaller, more manageable components, identifying patterns or trends, and applying relevant concepts or principles to devise solutions. Practice solving a variety of problems to develop adaptive problem-solving skills.
5. Creative Thinking: Encourage creative thinking and innovative approaches to problem-solving, as competitive exams often require students to think outside the box and devise unique solutions to challenging problems.
6. Practice with Sample Questions: Practice solving sample questions and past exam papers to familiarize yourself with the format, style, and types of questions commonly encountered in competitive exams. This helps build confidence and proficiency in critical thinking and problem-solving.

7. Time Management: Effective time management is crucial during competitive exams. Allocate sufficient time to read and understand each question, analyze the information provided, and devise a systematic approach to solving problems while keeping an eye on the time remaining.
8. Seek Clarification: If you encounter unclear or ambiguous questions, don't hesitate to seek clarification from the exam invigilator or use logical reasoning to interpret the question based on the available information.
9. Review and Reflect: After completing practice questions or mock exams, review your answers critically, identify any errors or misconceptions, and reflect on your problem-solving strategies. Learn from your mistakes and refine your approach to improve performance in future exams.

By honing their critical thinking and problem-solving skills, students can enhance their performance in competitive exams and develop valuable competencies that are essential for success in academia and beyond.

AUTHOR'S NOTE

THE PERSON WHO IS NOT COURAGEOUS ENOUGH TO TAKE RISK IN LIFE, WILL ACCOMPLISH NOTHING.... BECAUSE OPPORTUNITIES ARE CREATED...

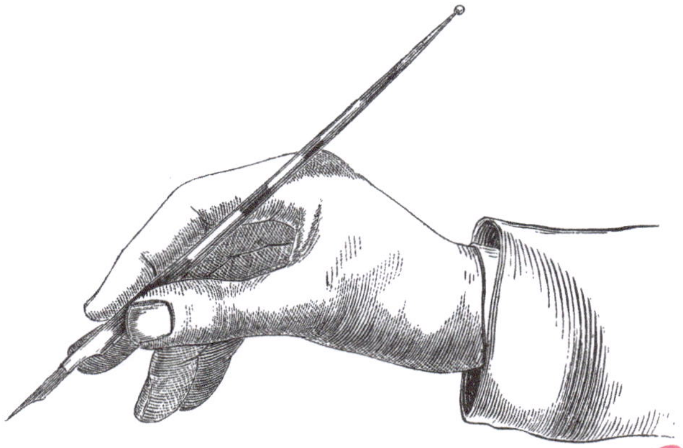

SUCCESS IS NOT ALWAYS ABOUT GREATNESS...
IT'S ABOUT CONSISTENCY...

Thank you...

hoping that this book will be helping the students to get into their right path of success...

Aadya. L

Head of the platform

Aadya Dr@ Pharm-D

Mail: draadyakims@gmail.com

9 789362 614551

Printed at Repro India Ltd.